W9-ABB-882

10|21

CELEBRATING HANUKKAH

BY TRUDI STRAIN TRUEIT · ILLUSTRATED BY REBECCA THORNBURGH

The Child's World®
childsworld.com

Published by The Child's World®
1980 Lookout Drive • Mankato, MN 56003-1705
800-599-READ • www.childsworld.com

ISBN 9781503853942 (Reinforced Library Binding)
ISBN 9781503854673 (Portable Document Format)
ISBN 9781503855052 (Online Multi-user eBook)
LCCN: 2021930092

Printed in the United States of America

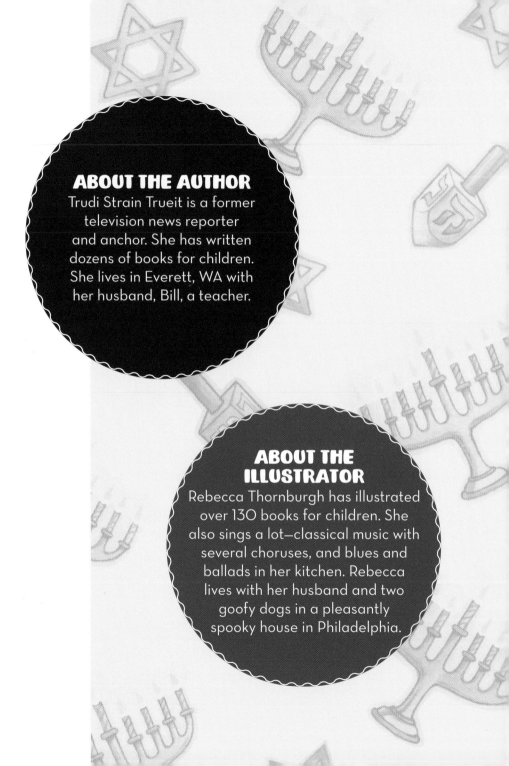

ABOUT THE AUTHOR

Trudi Strain Trueit is a former television news reporter and anchor. She has written dozens of books for children. She lives in Everett, WA with her husband, Bill, a teacher.

ABOUT THE ILLUSTRATOR

Rebecca Thornburgh has illustrated over 130 books for children. She also sings a lot—classical music with several choruses, and blues and ballads in her kitchen. Rebecca lives with her husband and two goofy dogs in a pleasantly spooky house in Philadelphia.

CONTENTS

CHAPTER 1

Happy Hanukkah

As the sun goes down, a Jewish family gathers around a candleholder. It is called a **menorah** (muh-NOR-uh). They greet each other with "Happy Hanukkah (HAHN-uh-kuh)!" People who are Jewish celebrate Hanukkah. The holiday lasts for eight days in December. The dates change every year.

Hanukkah is a joyful celebration filled with songs, food, and games. Why? To remember a **miracle** that happened long ago.

December is the time to celebrate the miracle of Hanukkah.

CHAPTER 2

A Miracle Happened There!

In **ancient** Israel, a Greek king named Antiochus (an-TY-uh-kuhs) outlawed the Jewish religion. Antiochus' army took over the Jewish **temple** in Jerusalem. Mattathias (ma-tuh-THY-uhs) was a Jewish priest. He and his sons formed an army to fight back. They were called the Maccabees (MAK-uh-beez).

The Maccabees were no match for the powerful Greek army. Yet, they won the battle.

Maccabees means "men as strong as hammers" in Hebrew, the ancient language of the Jewish people.

The Festival of Lights lasted for eight days while the oil burned nonstop in the lamp.

The Jewish people wanted to rededicate their temple to God. *Hanukkah* is the Hebrew word for "dedication." The menorah was supposed to burn nonstop during the festival. But it had only enough oil for one day. Miraculously, the lamp burned for eight days! The eight days of Hanukkah celebrate the eight days that the lamp burned.

Hanukkah is also called the Festival of Lights or the Feast of Dedication.

CHAPTER 3

Lights of the Season

The menorah is an important **symbol** of Hanukkah. Starting with the candle on the far right, it is lit each night during the holiday to honor the miracle of the lamp that burned for eight days.

A menorah holds eight candles, plus a ninth candle in the center. The center candle is the *shamash*. The shamash is used only to light the other candles. Special blessings are said when the shamash is lit.

Ancient menorahs were made of clay. Today, menorahs are made from many things, like sea shells, marshmallows, and even hammer handles.

On the first night of Hanukkah, someone lights the first candle on the far right of the menorah. On the second night, two candles are lit. This continues until the eighth night when all the candles are flickering.

In many families, it is **tradition** for everyone to take a turn lighting the menorah.

Lighting the menorah is a special part of Hanukkah.

CHAPTER 4

Fun and Games

Long ago, Jewish people dared to study their religion, although it was against the law. When they spotted Greek soldiers, they put their books away and pretended to play a game called *dreidel* (DRAY-duhl). A dreidel is a spinning top with four sides. Each side is marked with a Hebrew letter. Together, the letters stand for, "A great miracle happened there."

I Have a Little Dreidel

I have a little dreidel,
I made it out of clay.
And when it's dry and ready,
Then dreidel I shall play!
Oh dreidel, dreidel, dreidel,
I made it out of clay.
And when it's dry and ready,
Then dreidel I shall play!

Playing dreidel helped Jewish people safely study their religion.

Dreidel is still played today as part of the Hanukkah celebration.

Today, dreidel is a popular Hanukkah game. Here's how to play: Each player puts a penny or piece of candy in the main pile. Everyone takes turns spinning the dreidel. The letter you land on tells you what to do. *Nun* means do nothing. *Gimmel* lets you take all of the main pile. *Heh* means take half the pile. *Shin* means you have to put in another penny or piece of candy from your pile. When one person has all of the loot, he or she is the winner!

CHAPTER 5

Tasty Treats

It's tradition to eat foods fried in oil during Hanukkah. Why? To remember the oil that lasted eight days in the lamp.

Fried potato pancakes called *latkes* (LOT-kuhs) are popular. They may be served with sour cream or apple sauce.

Jelly donuts, or *sufganiyot* (soof-gahn-YOTE), are also a favorite Hanukkah treat. After they are fried, the donuts are dusted with powdered sugar or cinnamon.

It's fun to make butter cookies in the shapes of menorahs and dreidels for Hanukkah.

Many tasty Hanukkah treats are fried in oil.

CHAPTER 6

Come Celebrate!

During Hanukkah, people go to parties, festivals, and parades. They put on plays to reenact the battle of the Maccabees. Hanukkah is a time to be grateful for religious freedom and the right to practice your own beliefs.

It is also a time to think of others. Children may give clothes they have outgrown to a charity or volunteer to help neighbors. *Tzedakah* (tsi-DUH-kuh) is the Hebrew word for giving to those in need.

Some families exchange gifts during Hanukkah. Does your family have a special Hanukkah tradition?

Gelt is a traditional Hanukkah gift of chocolate or gold coins.

Some families put on a play for Hanukkah to remember the Maccabees.

CHAPTER 7

Poetry Corner

LET'S LIGHT THE MENORAH

Let's light the menorah
For the Festival of Lights,
One candle every evening
For eight great, joyous nights.

Latkes, games, and sharing,
Happiness and cheer.
Let's light the menorah
For Hanukkah is here.

FIVE LITTLE DREIDELS

Five little dreidels spinning in a row.
The first one spun, oh, so slow.
The second one went round and round.
The third one fell down on the ground.
The fourth one spun like a happy top.
The fifth one said, "I'll never stop!"
Five little dreidels, look and see,
Spinning at Hanukkah for you and me.

CHAPTER 8

Songs of Hanukkah

MAOZ TZUR (ROCK OF AGES)

This song is usually sung after reciting the
Hanukkah blessings and lighting the candles.

In Hebrew:
Ma'oz tsur y'shuati
l'ha nae l'shabeah.
Tikon bet t'filati
v'sham toda n'zabeah.
L'et tahin matbeah
mitzar ham'nabeah,
Az egmor b'shir mizmor,
hanukat hamizbeah.

In English:
Rock of ages, let our song
Praise Your saving power;
You, amid the raging foes,
Were our sheltering tower.
Furious they assailed us,
But Your arm availed us,
And Your word,
Broke their sword,
When our own strength failed us.

SEVIVON, SOV, SOV, SOV

In Hebrew:
Sevivon, sov, sov, sov
Chanukah, hu chag tov
Chanukah, hu chag tov
Sevivon, sov, sov, sov!
Chag simcha hu la-am
Nes gadol haya sham
Nes gadol haya sham
Chag simcha hu la-am.

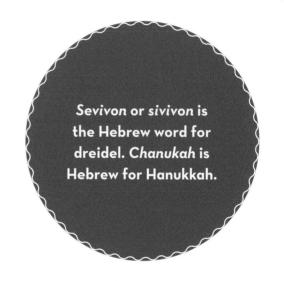

Sevivon or *sivivon* is the Hebrew word for dreidel. *Chanukah* is Hebrew for Hanukkah.

In English:
Dreidel, spin, spin, spin.
Hanukkah is a great holiday.
It is a celebration for our nation.
A great miracle happened there.

HANUKKAH, OH HANUKKAH

Hanukkah, oh Hanukkah, come light the Menorah.
Let's have a party, we'll all dance the hora.
Gather 'round the table, we'll all have a treat,
Sivivon to play with, and latkes to eat.
And while we are playing,
The candles are burning bright.
One for each night, they shed a sweet light,
To remind us of days long ago.
One for each night, they shed a sweet light,
To remind us of days long ago.

The *hora* is a traditional dance done at many different celebrations, including Hanukkah. Everyone moves clockwise in a circle, usually taking three steps forward and then one step back.

JOINING IN THE SPIRIT OF HANUKKAH

* Imagine what it must have been like for the Jewish in ancient times when they weren't allowed to study their religion. Talk with your family about the importance of being able to freely practice religious beliefs.

* Are you Jewish? What do you love to do for Hanukkah? If you're not Jewish, ask a Jewish friend what he or she does to celebrate The Festival of Lights.

* Talk to a parent or grandparent about their childhood Hanukkah memories.

* Gather your friends and siblings to play a game of dreidel (you can even make your own dreidel).

* Candles are lit during Hanukkah to symbolize light in the darkness. Think of some ways you can be a light to someone, like helping a new student at school or raking leaves for an elderly neighbor.

MAKING SWEET POTATO LATKES

What you need:
1 pound sweet potatoes, peeled and coarsely grated
2 scallions, finely chopped
1/3 cup all-purpose flour
2 large eggs, lightly beaten
1 teaspoon salt
1/2 teaspoon black pepper
3/4 cup vegetable oil
Sour cream or applesauce

Directions

1. Stir together potatoes, scallions, flour, eggs, salt, and pepper. Heat oil* in a large, deep skillet over moderately high heat.

2. Spoon about 1/3 cup potato mixture per latke into the oil, leaving plenty of room around each.

3. Use the spatula to flatten the latkes into 3-inch wide circles.

4. Reduce heat to moderate and cook until golden, about 2 minutes on each side.

5. Transfer latkes with spatula to paper towels to drain.

6. Serve the warm latkes with sour cream or applesauce.

*Have an adult help you operate the stove.

BUILDING A MENORAH

What you need:
9 cardboard tubes
Paint and brushes
Tape
Markers
Long piece of cardboard
Red, orange, and yellow tissue paper

Directions

1. Cut a little bit (about half an inch) off eight of the tubes.

2. Decorate all nine tubes either by covering them with construction paper, painting them, or coloring with markers. (Blue and silver are traditional colors.) Feel free to use glitter, too. You can also draw the Star of David on the center tube.

3. The cardboard will be the base of the menorah. Place all nine tubes on the base, with the tallest one in the middle and four shorter ones on each side.

4. Glue the tubes to the base. (You can also stick them into a piece of foam.)

5. Decorate the base to match.

6. Tear apart the tissue paper and insert various colors into the top of each tube to represent the flame of a candle.

GLOSSARY

ancient (AYN-shunt)—very old; usually meaning thousands of years

menorah (men-OR-uh)—a special candleholder used to celebrate Hanukkah

miracle (MEER-uh-kull)—a wondrous event with no human explanation

symbol (SIM-bull)—an object, image, or word that stands for an idea

temple (TEM-pull)—a Jewish place of worship

tradition (truh-DISH-un)—a long-held custom or something people do every year

LEARN MORE

BOOKS

Adler, David A. *The Story of Hanukkah*. New York, NY: Holiday House, 2013.

Heiligman, Deborah. *Holidays Around the World: Celebrate Hanukkah: With Light, Latkes, and Dreidels*. Washington, DC: National Geographic, 2016.

Olitzky, Kerry M. and Jesse Olitzky. *The Littlest Candle: A Hanukkah Story*. Moosic, PA: Kalanoit Books, 2020.

Perl, Erica S. *The Ninth Night of Hanukkah*. New York, NY: Sterling Children's Books, 2020.

Wing, Natasha. *The Night Before Hanukkah*. New York, NY: Grosset & Dunlap, 2014.

WEBSITES

Visit our website for links about Hanukkah and other holidays:
childsworld.com/links

Note to Parents, Teachers, and Librarians: We routinely verify our Web links to make sure they are safe and active sites. So encourage your readers to check them out!

INDEX